ULTIMATE CARS

Lamborghini

Rob Scott Colson

Published in 2013 by Wayland

Copyright © Wayland 2013

Wayland
338 Euston Road
London NW1 3BH

Wayland Australia
Level 17/207 Kent Street
Sydney NSW 2000

Editor: Camilla Lloyd
Produced by Tall Tree Ltd
Editor, Tall Tree: Emma Marriott
Designer: Jonathan Vipond

British Library Cataloguing in Publication Data

Colson, Robert Scott.
    Lamborghini. -- (Ultimate cars)
    1. Lamborghini automobile--Juvenile literature.
    I. Title II. Series
    629.2'222-dc22

ISBN: 978 0 7502 7222 3

Printed in China

Wayland is a division of Hachette Children's
Books, an Hachette UK company.

www.hachette.co.uk

Picture credits
All images Automobili Lamborghini Holding
S.p.A., except:
4 Geoff du Feu / Alamy

The website addresses (URLs) included in this
book were valid at the time of going to press.
However, because of the nature of the Internet,
it is possible that some addresses may have
changed, or sites may have changed or closed
down, since publication. While the author and
Publisher regret any inconvenience this may
cause the readers, no responsibility for any such
changes can be accepted by either the author or
the Publisher.

Contents

Lamborghini

The Lamborghini car company was founded in 1963 by Ferruccio Lamborghini, a tractor manufacturer who collected sports cars. He thought that all his cars had something wrong with their design.

Ferruccio decided he would build 'a very normal, but perfect' sports car. But many of the cars his company have made have been far from normal. They are some of the fastest cars ever allowed on the road.

Lamborghini made his fortune selling tractors such as this one, which is used to clean beaches in Tunisia.

Ferruccio Lamborghini sits on his personal Lamborghini, a Jarama GTS, outside the tractor factory in the early 1970s.

Amazing design

At the end of World War II, a young Ferruccio Lamborghini (1916–93) started making tractors out of abandoned military vehicles. By the 1960s, he was a rich man who owned many expensive cars. He wasn't happy with the Ferrari he owned, so he ordered his engineers to take it apart and see what was wrong with it. It was then that he decided he could make better cars himself.

Charging bull

The Lamborghini logo is a golden bull. It was chosen to represent Ferruccio Lamborghini's birth sign, Taurus the bull. Many of the company's cars have been named after famous bulls from bullfights in Spain. Lamborghini thought that the name of a fierce bull was a good match for his fast cars.

The charging bull is golden yellow. Many Lamborghinis are painted the same colour.

Murciélago

The Murciélago is a maximum-performance sports car, which means that it can reach very fast speeds and accelerate (increase speed) very quickly.

The latest model of the Murciélago is the LP640. The LP640 is available as a coupé with a fixed roof, and as a roadster with a removable roof. The coupé version is featured here.

Every part of the body is designed to be as aerodynamic as possible.

Amazing design

When a car moves, it needs to force the air in front of it out of the way. This causes drag – a combination of air resistance and friction between the car and the air, which slows the car down. The Murciélago's 'wedge' shape is aerodynamic because it allows the car to cut a path through the air at high speeds, reducing drag. This shape was originally developed for fighter jets.

The engine's 12 cylinders are arranged in two groups of six in a 'V' shape.

STATS AND FACTS

YEARS OF PRODUCTION **2006–present**
ENGINE SIZE **6.5 litre**
NUMBER OF CYLINDERS **12**
TRANSMISSION **Manual**
GEARBOX **6-speed**
0–100 KPH (0–62 MPH) **3.4 seconds**
TOP SPEED **340 kph**
WEIGHT (KG) **1665**
CO_2 EMISSIONS (G/KM) **495**
FUEL ECONOMY (L/100 KM) **21.3 (13.2 mpg)**

Engine

The Murciélago has an enormous 6.5-litre engine – four times bigger than the engine of a normal family car. This powerful engine is cooled by a Variable Air-flow Cooling System, which opens to let air in from outside the car during hot conditions.

Reventón

This is a car for millionaires – literally – as it costs 1 million euros. It has the same engine as the Murciélago, but is modelled even more closely on fighter jets.

In 2007, a Reventón raced against a Tornado jet plane on a 3 km-long runway in Brescia, Italy. The car led the race almost to the end, but the jet fighter overtook it in the last few metres.

Style and function

Every feature of the Reventón is designed to look great and perform brilliantly. Stylish carbon fins are screwed onto the aluminium spokes of each wheel. The car's brakes squeeze the wheels with ceramic brake discs. This creates friction and makes the wheels very hot. The fins create a turbine effect as the wheels spin, drawing air over the brake discs to cool them down.

G-Force Meter shows the stresses on the car as it takes corners.

Screens to left and right display essential information such as speed and fuel levels.

Amazing design

Three liquid crystal displays inside the car show a variety of information from the on-board computer to the driver. The screen in the middle, known as the G-Force Meter, is unique to the Reventón. On a 3D grid, the meter shows the gravitational forces as the car accelerates or goes around bends. This means that the driver knows at all times exactly what stress the car is under. Both Formula 1 cars and aircraft use similar instruments to ensure that drivers or pilots do not lose control at high speeds.

The Reventón is a very exclusive car. Just 21 cars have been made – one for the Lamborghini museum and 20 for sale. Each one is stamped inside with its own number between 0 and 20.

Side air intakes help to cool the ceramic brake discs.

STATS AND FACTS

YEARS OF PRODUCTION
2008–present
ENGINE SIZE **6.5 litre**
NUMBER OF CYLINDERS **12**
TRANSMISSION **Manual**
GEARBOX **6-speed**
0–100 KPH (0–62 MPH) **3.4 seconds**
TOP SPEED **340 kph**
WEIGHT (KG) **1665**
CO_2 EMISSIONS (G/KM) **495**
FUEL ECONOMY (L/100 KM) **21.3 (13.2 mpg)**

Gallardo Spyder

The Gallardo was first produced in 2003 as a coupé, a car with a fixed, hard roof. In 2006, Lamborghini produced the Gallardo Spyder, which has a soft roof.

The Spyder's chassis (the car's 'skeleton') has been reinforced (made stronger) to make up for its lack of a hard roof. This change means that it is a little heavier and slower than the coupé.

Retracting roof

The roof of the Gallardo Spyder can be removed at the touch of a button. The engine cover lifts up and the soft top folds back into a space next to the engine behind the seats. The engine cover and the soft roof are both controlled by rams – rods that move out and in. The rams are hydraulic, which means that they are powered by liquid under pressure.

Engine cover

Soft roof

STATS AND FACTS

YEARS OF PRODUCTION **2006–present**

ENGINE SIZE **5 litre**

NUMBER OF CYLINDERS **10**

TRANSMISSION **Semi-automatic**

GEARBOX **6-speed**

0–100 KPH (0–62 MPH) **4.3 seconds**

TOP SPEED **314 kph roof closed; 307 kph roof open**

WEIGHT (KG) **1570**

CO_2 EMISSIONS (G/KM) **400**

FUEL ECONOMY (L/100 KM) **18.1 (15.6 mpg)**

The chassis is made of a space frame – a lightweight structure of metal rods fixed to each other in a grid pattern.

Amazing design

The spoiler lies flat against the boot at low speeds.

The Gallardo has the distinctive Lamborghini wedge shape that is so aerodynamic it is in danger of taking off at high speed! To solve this problem, the rear spoiler (a bar at the back of the car) automatically rises up when the car's speed reaches 120 kph. The spoiler disrupts (spoils) the flow of air over the car, producing downforce that keeps the wheels safely on the road.

350 GT

The 350 was Lamborghini's first car. It was called the 350 because its engine was 350 cubic centimetres in size.

The 350 produced to sell to the public was called the 350 GT. Only 120 350 GTs were ever made, but it is the car that established Lamborghini as a new and exciting car manufacturer.

Amazing design

One of the most amazing parts of the 350's design cannot be seen from the outside. The chassis was made using a frame of thin metal tubes. The tubes were then covered in aluminium panels. Most cars at that time were made using thicker tubes. The technique was called *superleggera* (an Italian word meaning 'super light'), and it made the car lighter and faster.

GT stands for 'grand tourer' – a high-performance car designed to be driven over long distances.

The very first 350 was called the GTV. It was a prototype – a model made to show how the design would work. It looked the part but it did not have an engine!

Dream team

One of the keys to the 350's success was the team behind it. Its chief engineer, Giotto Bizzarrini, had been chief designer for rival Italian company Ferrari. The designer, Gian Paolo Dallara, later went on to found his own company, and makes the chassis for all IndyCar racing cars today.

STATS AND FACTS

YEARS OF PRODUCTION **1964-66**
ENGINE SIZE **3.5 litre**
NUMBER OF CYLINDERS **12**
TRANSMISSION **Manual**
GEARBOX **5-speed**
0–100 KPH (0–62 MPH) **6.5 seconds**
TOP SPEED **250 kph**
WEIGHT (KG) **1200**
CO_2 EMISSIONS (G/KM) **Not available**
FUEL ECONOMY (L/100 KM) **Not available**

Miura

The Miura replaced the 350 GT, and was the first Lamborghini model to have a name inspired by bullfighting. The Miura was named after a Spanish breeder of fighting bulls called Antonio Miura. It had a larger engine than the 350, and could go 30 kph faster.

The engines in the very first Miuras would sometimes catch fire when the car accelerated, but once they had fixed this dangerous problem, it became a hugely successful model.

Unusually, the Miura's bonnet opens down the middle. The front and rear panels open up like a clam shell.

Amazing design

The Miura was one of the first two-seater road cars to have the engine in the middle of the car rather than at the front. This spread the car's weight and made it easier to control at high speed. Before the Miura, only racing cars had been made this way. It was not surprising that the Miura was the fastest street-legal car of its time.

Lamborghini improved the engine in later models, making them even faster.

Only one Miura Roadster was ever made, but some owners have converted their Miuras to look like it.

Open top

In 1968, Lamborghini built a roadster version of the Miura. Only one was ever made. It does not have a removable roof like the Gallardo Spyder. In fact, it does not have a roof at all. This one-off car was shown at motor shows, but it was decided not to make any more – possibly because its owners would want to be able to drive in the rain too!

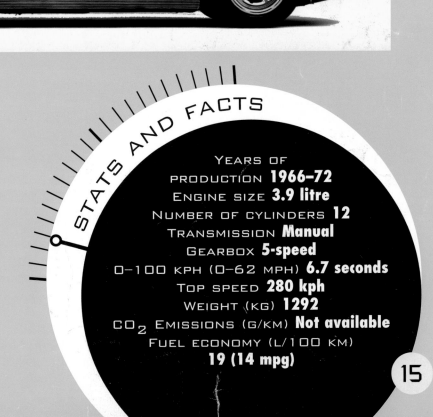

STATS AND FACTS

YEARS OF PRODUCTION **1966–72**
ENGINE SIZE **3.9 litre**
NUMBER OF CYLINDERS **12**
TRANSMISSION **Manual**
GEARBOX **5-speed**
0–100 KPH (0–62 MPH) **6.7 seconds**
TOP SPEED **280 kph**
WEIGHT (KG) **1292**
CO_2 EMISSIONS (G/KM) **Not available**
FUEL ECONOMY (L/100 KM)
19 (14 mpg)

Countach

The Countach was the first Lamborghini to be designed with the now-familiar wedge shape.

The shape was the idea of designer Marcello Gandini. It looks very sleek, but its sharp corners are in fact not as aerodynamic as Lamborghini's later wedge-shaped cars, whose designers used wind tunnels and computers to perfect the shape.

Lamborghini have attached 'scissor' doors to all their wedge-shaped cars.

Amazing design

At just over 2 metres across, the Countach is 20–30 centimetres wider than most road cars, which could cause problems on narrow streets. Its 'scissor' doors open up rather than out, like a bird raising its wings, so there is room to climb in and out. The doors swing open from a hinge at the front – an arrangement known as a 'jack-knife'.

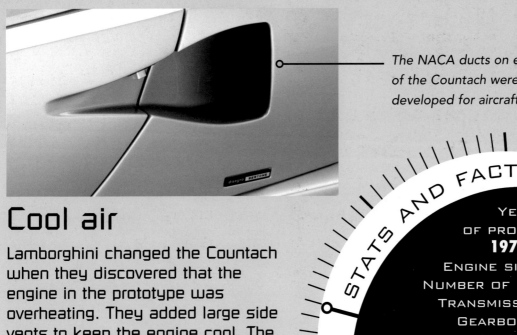

The NACA ducts on either side of the Countach were originally developed for aircraft.

Cool air

Lamborghini changed the Countach when they discovered that the engine in the prototype was overheating. They added large side vents to keep the engine cool. The vents are known as NACA (National Advisory Panel for Aeronautics) ducts. The ducts do not stick out, so they allow air to be drawn in over the engine without damaging the car's aerodynamics.

The Countach made the sharp-angled style popular.

STATS AND FACTS

YEARS
OF PRODUCTION
1974–89
ENGINE SIZE **3.9 litre**
NUMBER OF CYLINDERS **12**
TRANSMISSION **Manual**
GEARBOX **5-speed**
0–100 KPH (0–62 MPH) **5.9 seconds**
TOP SPEED **300 kph**
WEIGHT (KG) **1200**
CO_2 EMISSIONS (G/KM) **Not available**
FUEL ECONOMY (L/100 KM)
25.7 (11 mpg)

Diablo

The Countach was designed for style. But the model that replaced it, the Diablo, was made for speed.

Its name suits it well – *diablo* is the Spanish word for devil, and this car can go devilishly fast. It is also devilishly noisy, and you are likely to hear a Diablo long before you see it. Its engine roars at over 100 decibels – as loud as your MP3 player turned up to full volume.

Amazing design

The cockpit of the Diablo is pushed forward to allow room for the enormous 6-litre engine that sits behind it. This means there is not much leg room for the driver or passenger. There are also very few luxuries in the Diablo as each new gadget would add weight to the car and reduce its speed. With a top speed of 338 kph, the Diablo could give a Formula 1 car a good race.

Racing devil

In 1994, to celebrate the 30th anniversary of Lamborghini's first car, the company made a special racing version of the Diablo known as the SE30. The SE30 had even fewer luxuries than the standard Diablo. It had no radio, air-conditioning or sound insulation and was fitted with carbon fibre seats. This made it 125 kg lighter than the standard model – a thrilling, if noisy, hot and uncomfortable drive.

In 1999, Lamborghini redesigned the body of the Diablo slightly and gave it a bigger engine. The result was the Diablo GT, the fastest sports car in the world at the time.

STATS AND FACTS

Years of production **1990–2001**
Engine size **6 litre**
Number of cylinders **12**
Transmission **Manual**
Gearbox **5-speed**
0–100 kph (0–62 mph) **3.5 seconds**
Top speed **338 kph**
Weight (kg) **1460**
CO_2 Emissions (g/km) **Not available**
Fuel economy (l/100 km) **24 (12 mpg)**

Racing

Perhaps surprisingly for a manufacturer of some of the fastest cars ever made, Ferruccio Lamborghini decided that motor racing was too expensive.

After Ferrucio retired, the company became involved in Formula 1 as an engine supplier. Finally, after Lamborghini's death, racing models of the Diablo competed in the Diablo Supertrophy, a race series that was held from 1996 to 1999.

A racing Diablo, the first car made entirely by Lamborghini to compete on the track.

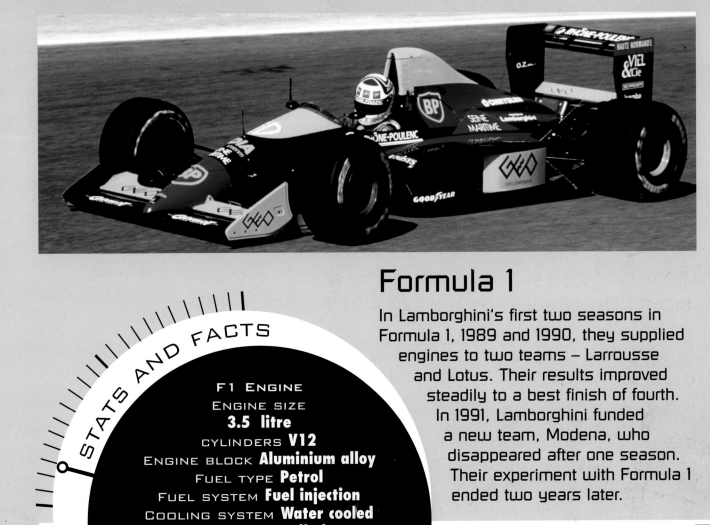

Formula 1

In Lamborghini's first two seasons in Formula 1, 1989 and 1990, they supplied engines to two teams – Larrousse and Lotus. Their results improved steadily to a best finish of fourth. In 1991, Lamborghini funded a new team, Modena, who disappeared after one season. Their experiment with Formula 1 ended two years later.

STATS AND FACTS

F1 Engine
ENGINE SIZE
3.5 litre
CYLINDERS **V12**
ENGINE BLOCK **Aluminium alloy**
FUEL TYPE **Petrol**
FUEL SYSTEM **Fuel injection**
COOLING SYSTEM **Water cooled**
VALVES **4 per cylinder**

Cylinders

Spark plugs ignite (set fire to) the fuel

Engine block – a solid frame in which the cylinders pump up and down.

Amazing design

Lamborghini developed the powerful 12-cylinder, 3.5-litre engine used in Formula 1 in partnership with the US company Chrysler. However, the continuous changes that Formula 1 demands, as the drivers push the cars to their limits, proved too expensive for Lamborghini.

Glossary

aerodynamic
Shaped to minimize air resistance when moving at high speed.

chassis
The frame or skeleton of the car to which the body and the engine are attached.

coupé
A car with a hard roof that cannot be removed.

cubic centimetre (cc)
A unit of measurement used to describe the size of an engine. There are 1000 cubic centimetres in 1 litre.

cylinder
An engine chamber where pistons pump up and down, producing the engine's power.

drag
A force caused by air resistance that slows a car down when it moves.

engine block
The solid metal base of the engine in which the cylinders are housed.

fuel economy
The rate at which a car uses fuel. It is measured in litres per 100 kilometres or miles per gallon.

fuel injection
A way of adding fuel to the engine by mixing the fuel with air under pressure before injecting it into the cylinders.

gear
A system of cogs that transfer power from the engine to the wheels. Low gears give extra power for acceleration or driving uphill. High gears are used for faster speeds.

performance
A measurement of a car's power and handling. A car that accelerates quickly and has a high top speed is said to be high-performance.

prototype
An experimental model made to test a design before it goes into production.

roadster
A two-seater car with a removable roof, also called a convertible.

spark plug
A device inside a cylinder that makes a spark to ignite (set fire to) the fuel.

transmission
The way in which a car transfers power from the engine to the wheels, via a gearbox that allows the driver to change gear.

variable air-flow cooling system
A system that cools the engine by taking in air from outside the car. The air intake opens in hot conditions, but closes in colder weather.

wedge
An object that is thick at one end, and narrows to a thin edge at the other.

Models at a glance

Model	Years Made	Numbers Built	Did You Know?
350 GT	1964–66	120	As Lamborghini's pioneering model, the 350 GT provided Ferrari with a serious Italian competitor.
Miura	1966–72	764	With its mid-engined layout, this trend-leading car set the standard for two-seater high-performance cars.
Jarama	1970–76	328	Created for the 'gentleman', this was one of Ferruccio Lamborghini's favourite models.
Countach	1974–89	2042	Its innovative wedge-shape body is only 1.07 metres tall – a design that has redefined the look of sports cars.
Diablo	1990–2001	3000	In 1999, the Diablo GT was the world's fastest sports car with a top speed of 338 kph.
Murciélago	2001–present	3066 (at the end of 2007)	To show off its 6.5-litre engine, the LP640 can be supplied with a transparent glass engine hood.
Gallardo	2003–present	6801 (at the end of 2007)	The LP 560-4 Spyder takes only 4 seconds to sprint from 0 to 100 kph.
Reventón	2008–present	21 (at the end of 2008)	The on-board computer features the G-Force Meter which is also used by aircraft and is unique to this model.

Websites

www.lamborghini.com

The official website of the company, with pictures, news and technical information about all their models, past and present.

www.sportscarcup.com

...e that compares sports cars of different makes. ...hotos and a short history of each model.

www.topgear.com

The website of the popular BBC TV series, with reviews, interactive games and a special feature on the history of Lamborghini.

www.lambocars.com

The online version of *Lamborghini Cars* magazine where enthusiasts chat about all things Lamborghini.

→Index